BE HAPPY THAT...

BE HAPPY THAT...

This Book Isn't Coated in Poison, Plus 100 *Other Reasons to* CHEER UP

Melissa Heckscher
Jordan Burchette
Pat Mellon

Illustrations by Del Thorpe

CLARKSON POTTER PUBLISHERS
New York

 A QUIRK PACKAGING BOOK

All rights reserved.
Published in the United States by Clarkson Potter/Publishers,
an imprint of the Crown Publishing Group,
a division of Random House, Inc., New York.
www.crownpublishing.com
www.clarksonpotter.com

CLARKSON POTTER is a trademark and POTTER with
colophon is a registered trademark of Random House, Inc.

Library of Congress Cataloging-in-Publication Data
is available upon request.

ISBN 978-0-307-46496-5

Printed in Singapore

Design by Lynne Yeamans

10 9 8 7 6 5 4 3 2 1

First Edition

The authors would like to thank all of the following whom/which make them happy:

Gravity; jalapeño peppers; parents (ours and others); Florida State football; samurai; Rod Stiffens; the messiahs of all major religions, including Thor, the Norse God of Thunder; the letter H; the number 27; Angus Young; macaroni and cheese; Jock Lauterer; the Santa Monica ferris wheel; David Letterman; Taylor Negron; the Ibanez Iceman; New Orleans; Gene Simmons; palindromes; Wilbur Wright; misery; Las Vegas; Largo, FL; Jenevieve; pizza; olives; Barstow; Noah; the color blue; steak-cut fries; make-believe things; that guy behind you; Hal's restaurant; and Pax.

And, of course, thanks to our editors, Sharyn Rosart and Erin Canning of Quirk Packaging; our illustrator, Del Thorpe; our designer, Lynne Yeamans; and our publisher, Clarkson Potter.

Being happy rocks.

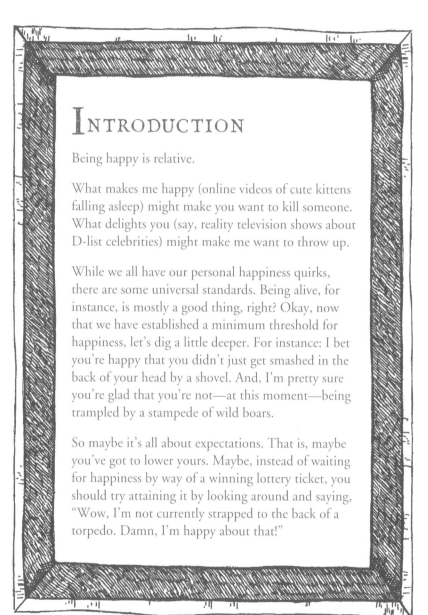

INTRODUCTION

Being happy is relative.

What makes me happy (online videos of cute kittens falling asleep) might make you want to kill someone. What delights you (say, reality television shows about D-list celebrities) might make me want to throw up.

While we all have our personal happiness quirks, there are some universal standards. Being alive, for instance, is mostly a good thing, right? Okay, now that we have established a minimum threshold for happiness, let's dig a little deeper. For instance: I bet you're happy that you didn't just get smashed in the back of your head by a shovel. And, I'm pretty sure you're glad that you're not—at this moment—being trampled by a stampede of wild boars.

So maybe it's all about expectations. That is, maybe you've got to lower yours. Maybe, instead of waiting for happiness by way of a winning lottery ticket, you should try attaining it by looking around and saying, "Wow, I'm not currently strapped to the back of a torpedo. Damn, I'm happy about that!"

Still having a hard time getting to that happy place? *Be Happy That…* is here to help! With 101 completely absurd (yet hilarious) reasons to appreciate your life, this book is guaranteed to lower your happiness standards while improving your positive outlook on life. In other words: Read this, be happy.

Here's how to use this book:
1. Read an entry.
2. Admire the spot-on illustration.
3. Give yourself a moment to take in what you've read and seen.
4. Laugh (preferably, out loud).
5. Say to yourself, "So true, so true." Then, "Hey, things could definitely be worse!"

Being happy is easier than you thought, right? Now stop being so ambitious about your happiness and try smiling a little. Consider laughing at the absurdity of it all. Read this book over and over again until your friends start thinking you're crazy and you're so happy you don't even care.

If that doesn't work, try the sleepy kittens.

THE REASONS

BE HAPPY THAT...

you respond to gravity.

BE HAPPY THAT...

elevator music isn't live.

Be happy that...

you don't have to take making "eye contact" literally.

Be happy that...

you aren't a giant squid.

Be happy that...

you aren't suddenly
allergic to pants.

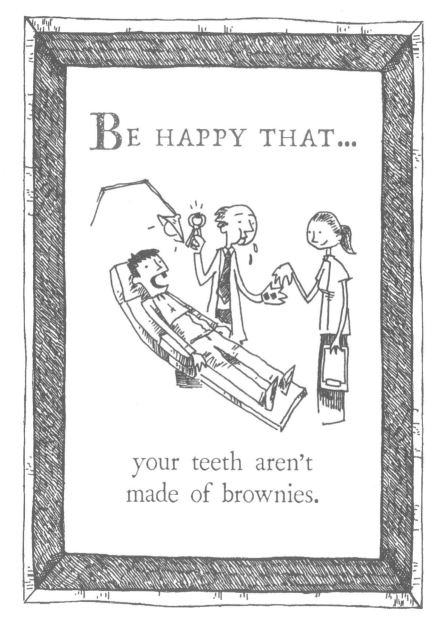

Be happy that...

your teeth aren't
made of brownies.

BE HAPPY THAT...

your stapler doesn't hate you.

BE HAPPY THAT...

you don't have antlers.

BE HAPPY THAT...

being happy doesn't
cause flatulence.

BE HAPPY THAT...

snow isn't hot.

BE HAPPY THAT...

you haven't been hollowed
out for use as a canoe.

Be happy that...

humans aren't descended
from the ostrich.

Be happy that...

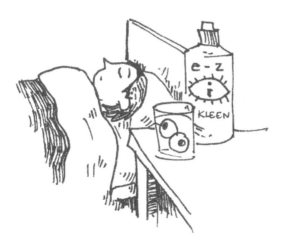

you don't have to
regularly eject and clean
your eyeballs.

BE HAPPY THAT...

people can't see thought bubbles over your head.

Be happy that...

you don't speak in whale calls.

BE HAPPY THAT...

you don't have to eat
regurgitated food.

BE HAPPY THAT...

blinking doesn't change the channel.

Be happy that...

your bike helmet
doesn't make contact with
the mother ship.

Be happy that...

all beaches aren't made
of quicksand.

BE HAPPY THAT...

you aren't sexually
attracted to bees.

Be happy that...

falling in love doesn't make you spontaneously combust.

Be happy that...

you're not naked on live television.

Be happy that...

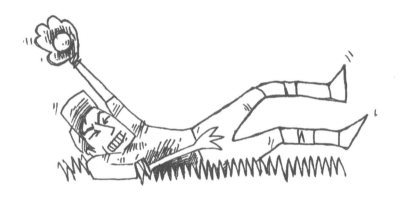

grass isn't sharp.

BE HAPPY THAT...

you come preassembled.

Be happy that...

this book isn't
coated in poison.

Be happy that...

you don't have a
nervous habit of eating
important papers.

BE HAPPY THAT...

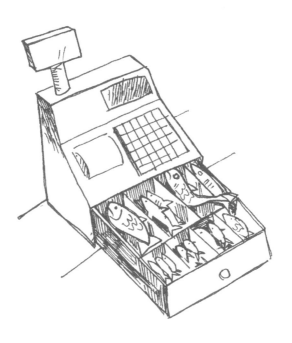

currency isn't fish.

BE HAPPY THAT...

you know the difference
between a fork and a stick
of burning dynamite.

BE HAPPY THAT...

a doggie door isn't the only
entrance to your house.

Be happy that...

drinking hot cocoa
doesn't make you invisible.

BE HAPPY THAT...

automatic weapons don't spontaneously appear in your bags whenever you go through a metal detector.

BE HAPPY THAT...

you no longer have to
bathe with your siblings.

Be happy that...

you know how
to sit down.

BE HAPPY THAT...

vampires don't work
at blood banks.

Be happy that...

your hairdresser
knows more than
one style.

BE HAPPY THAT...

your cell-phone ringer
isn't set to "electric shock."

Be happy that...

you don't sweat honey.

Be happy that...

the ground isn't out to get you.

Be happy that...

you don't call out your
PIN number in your sleep.

Be happy that...

sandwiches don't
contain witches.

BE HAPPY THAT...

you aren't solar powered.

Be happy that...

sharks can't hunt on land.

Be happy that...

your legs don't have a
mind of their own.

BE HAPPY THAT...

you're not a
deodorant inspector.

Be happy that...

cats have whiskers
instead of mustaches.

BE HAPPY THAT...

you don't have to work at keeping your head attached.

BE HAPPY THAT...

you don't have to play
a laugh track every time
you tell a joke.

Be happy that...

microscopic things stay
microscopic.

BE HAPPY THAT...

your car doesn't have a
sneeze-activated ejector seat.

BE HAPPY THAT...

hands are the body part
we customarily shake.

BE HAPPY THAT...

your computer doesn't require love and attention to work properly.

BE HAPPY THAT...

your body hair isn't made of needles.

BE HAPPY
THAT...

your eyebrows aren't
caterpillars.

BE HAPPY THAT...

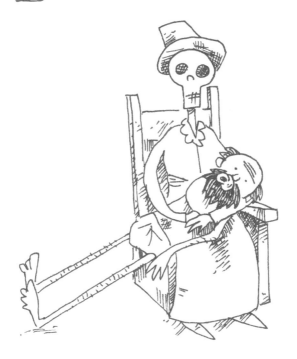

you don't age in photos.

BE HAPPY THAT...

stepping on your shadow
doesn't hurt.

BE HAPPY THAT...

Meep

you don't have to bathe
in kittens.

BE HAPPY THAT...

you don't get sucked
into your television during
harrowing moments.

BE HAPPY THAT...

pigeons don't mistake
your nose for a
giant breadcrumb.

BE HAPPY
THAT...

you don't attract
lightning.

BE HAPPY THAT...

you're not required to
sit on a stranger's lap on
a crowded train.

BE HAPPY THAT...

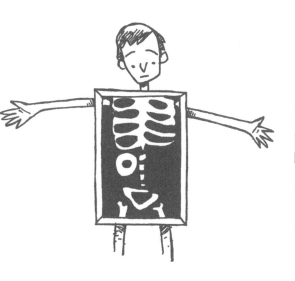

your liver hasn't been replaced by a donut.

BE HAPPY THAT...

your new neighbors
aren't cannibals.

Be happy that...

your respective cheeks
are in their existing
locations.

BE HAPPY THAT...

the family members of bugs
you've squashed don't seek
revenge while you're sleeping.

BE HAPPY THAT...

you don't mistake
small children
for parking meters.

Be happy that...

your great-grandmother
isn't the pilot
of your plane.

BE HAPPY THAT...

your pet can't talk
back to you.

Be happy that...

your house is always
in the same place when
you come home.

BE HAPPY THAT...

you're not a bulletproof
vest tester.

Be happy that...

a bird hasn't nested
in your hoodie.

BE HAPPY THAT...

you know the difference between an office chair and a toilet.

Be happy that...

you don't speak in
movie quotes.

BE HAPPY THAT...

you don't cry wasps.

BE HAPPY THAT...

you don't share a
cell-phone number
with Satan.

BE HAPPY THAT...

your necktie doesn't constrict every time you say, "um," in a meeting.

BE HAPPY THAT...

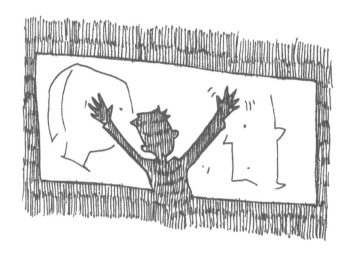

you don't have a habit
of involuntary arm-flailing
in movie theaters.

Be happy that...

bottled water doesn't
come with its own sea life.

BE HAPPY THAT...

your range of facial
expressions isn't limited
to emoticons.

Be happy that...

your trial lawyer
isn't a mime.

BE HAPPY THAT...

your roommate hasn't secretly outfitted your house with hidden cameras for a reality TV show.

BE HAPPY THAT...

the underwire in your bra doesn't receive CB transmissions.

BE HAPPY THAT...

your bottom
doesn't resemble an
archery target.

BE HAPPY THAT...

you don't have to
travel by mail.

BE HAPPY THAT...

your bathtub isn't located in a 24-hour convenience store.

BE HAPPY THAT...

you don't have to
keep an eye out
for zombies at funerals.

BE HAPPY
THAT...

your dog doesn't have a
gambling addiction.

BE HAPPY THAT...

you're not a
collector's item.

BE HAPPY THAT...

you don't have to style
your nose hair every day.

Be happy that...

you're immune to
computer viruses.

Be happy that...

you're not the first
janitor on the moon.

BE HAPPY THAT...

it's not Take Your Skunk
to Work Day.

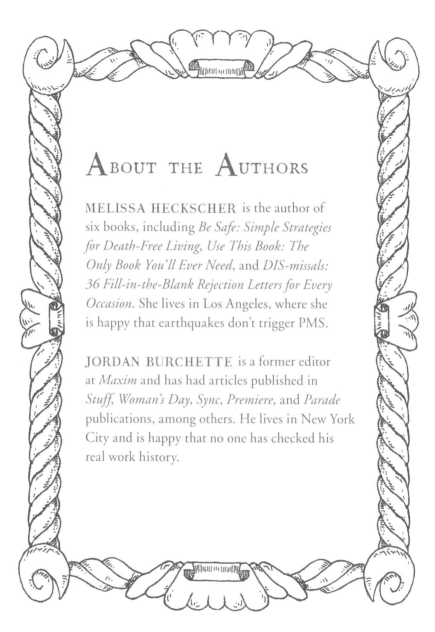

About the Authors

MELISSA HECKSCHER is the author of six books, including *Be Safe: Simple Strategies for Death-Free Living*, *Use This Book: The Only Book You'll Ever Need*, and *DIS-missals: 36 Fill-in-the-Blank Rejection Letters for Every Occasion*. She lives in Los Angeles, where she is happy that earthquakes don't trigger PMS.

JORDAN BURCHETTE is a former editor at *Maxim* and has had articles published in *Stuff*, *Woman's Day*, *Sync*, *Premiere*, and *Parade* publications, among others. He lives in New York City and is happy that no one has checked his real work history.

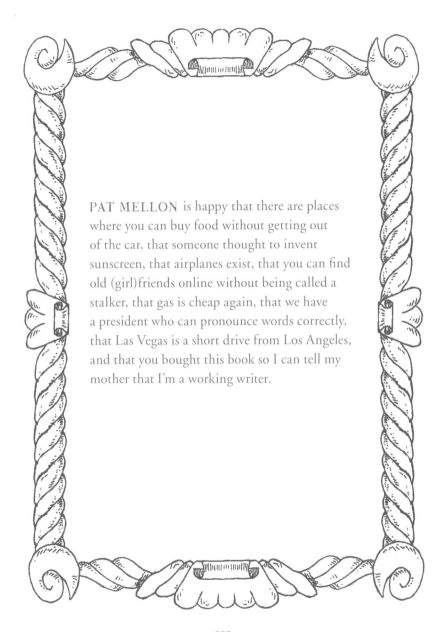

PAT MELLON is happy that there are places where you can buy food without getting out of the car, that someone thought to invent sunscreen, that airplanes exist, that you can find old (girl)friends online without being called a stalker, that gas is cheap again, that we have a president who can pronounce words correctly, that Las Vegas is a short drive from Los Angeles, and that you bought this book so I can tell my mother that I'm a working writer.

About the Illustrator

DEL THORPE is an illustrator who lives in Brighton, England. He is happy that he actually gets paid for drawing pictures.